*For Laura, who urged me to write a book
about my "hero," Beatrix Potter. Well—here it is!
Appreciatively, David*

Henry Holt and Company, LLC
Publishers since 1866
175 Fifth Avenue, New York, New York 10010
mackids.com

Henry Holt® is a registered trademark of Henry Holt and Company, LLC.
Copyright © 2015 by David McPhail
All rights reserved.

Library of Congress Cataloging-in-Publication Data
McPhail, David, 1940–
Beatrix Potter and her paint box / By David McPhail.—First edition.
pages   cm
ISBN 978-0-8050-9170-0 (hardcover)
1. Potter, Beatrix, 1866–1943—Juvenile literature. 2. Authors, English—20th century—Biography—
Juvenile literature. 3. Artists—Great Britain—Biography—Juvenile literature. I. Title.
PR6031.O72Z76 2015   823'.912—dc23   [B]   2015003703

Henry Holt books may be purchased for business or promotional use. For information on bulk
purchases, please contact the Macmillan Corporate and Premium Sales Department
at (800) 221-7945 x5442 or by e-mail at specialmarkets@macmillan.com.

First edition—2015 / Book designed by Véronique Lefèvre Sweet
The artist used watercolor and ink on illustration board to create the illustrations for this book.
Printed in China by RR Donnelley Asia Printing Solutions, Ltd.,
Dongguan City, Guangdong Province

1 3 5 7 9 10 8 6 4 2

Beatrix Potter
and Her Paint Box

DAVID McPHAIL

Henry Holt and Company   New York

Beatrix Potter was born on July 28, 1866, in London, England. Her parents were wealthy and, like most people of their class, were not heavily involved in raising their children. That task was left to nannies and tutors, who cared for and taught Beatrix in the upstairs nursery, away from the activities of the grown-ups.

Even as a little girl, Beatrix loved art.
She spent many happy hours at her grandparents'
home, looking at the paintings on the walls.

When she was still very young, Beatrix
was given her mother's paint box.

She made sketchbooks out of paper and string, and filled them with paintings of the things she saw around her.

She painted pictures of her pets . . .

. . . including a mouse named Henrietta, who once scampered across her paint box, leaving tracks everywhere!

Beatrix shared the nursery with her little brother, Bertram, who also loved art and animals. His pets included a bat, a lizard, and a snake.

Beatrix wanted to paint a picture of the snake, but before she could, it got away and was never found.

She painted the lizard instead.

In the summer, Beatrix and her family moved to the countryside. Even the animals came along!

Beatrix and Bertram loved the country. There was so much to do, and to see, and to paint.

Sometimes Beatrix went along with her
father on his fishing trips. While her father
fished, Beatrix painted.

She even discovered some rare toadstools
and painted pictures of them!

Bertram and Beatrix went out onto the lake in Bertram's small boat. While Bertram rowed . . . Beatrix painted.

When summer came to an end, the family returned to the city, and Bertram, like other boys his age, was sent off to school.

Beatrix missed him terribly. She painted more than ever to keep from becoming too sad.

One winter, Beatrix got very sick. She was so weak that she had to stay in bed for several months. She was even too ill to paint!

Gradually Beatrix got better, and she was able to paint again.

She was given painting lessons, but she preferred to paint in her own way, so the lessons stopped.

Every summer, when Bertram came home from
school, the whole family returned to the country.

It was where Beatrix was happiest.

Beatrix had her own pony cart, and she drove it all over the countryside, stopping now and then to paint.

Years passed. Beatrix was growing up. Even when she became a young woman, she continued to live with her parents and to spend summers in the country with them.

And she never stopped painting.

When she learned that the son of a friend had become ill, Beatrix recalled how dreary it was to be confined to bed. She wrote a story about a rabbit and drew some pictures to go with it. Then she sent the illustrated letter to the sick boy, Noel, to cheer him up.

The boy's mother urged Beatrix to make a book of the story, which she eventually did.

That story, "The Tale of Peter Rabbit,"
became a bestseller, and Beatrix went on to
write many more books for children.

Beatrix insisted that the books be small.
"Little books for little hands," she said.

Soon her stories became
famous all over the world.
The naughty Peter Rabbit,
the mischievous Tom
Kitten, and the adorable
Mrs. Tiggy-Winkle, as well
as the rest of Beatrix's
many characters, remain
popular to this very day.